The Let's Talk Library™

Let's Talk About When Your Parent Doesn't Speak English

Maureen K. Wittbold

The Rosen Publishing Group's
PowerKids Press™
New York

Published in 1997 by The Rosen Publishing Group, Inc.
29 East 21st Street, New York, NY 10010

First Edition

Book Design: Erin McKenna

Photo Illustrations: Cover and photo illustrations by Seth Dinnerman.

Wittbold, Maureen.
    Let's talk about when your parent doesn't speak English / Maureen K. Wittbold.
        p.   cm. (The let's talk library)
    Includes index.
    Summary: Briefly describes why a person's parent may not speak English, what effect this may have on a child, and how to handle this situation.
    ISBN 0-8239-5044-1
    1. Children of immigrants —United States—Juvenile literature. 2. Bilingualism in children—United States—Juvenile literature. 3. Parent and child—United States—Juvenile literature. 4. Acculturation—United States—Juvenile literature. 5. Americanizations—Juvenile literature. [1. Parent and child. 2. Bilingualism. 3. Immigrants.] I. Title. II. Series.
HQ792.U5W56 1997
306.874—dc21   96-53428
                                                                        CIP
                                                                        AC

Manufactured in the United States of America

Table of Contents

You're Not Alone

Do you have a parent who doesn't speak English? If you do, you are not alone. Thousands of people move to English-speaking countries every year. They bring with them the foods, **customs** (KUS-tumz), **traditions** (truh-DISH-unz), and languages of their homelands. There are nearly 40 million people living in the United States who think of English as a **foreign** (FOR-en) language. There are millions of kids who have one or two parents who don't speak English.

◄ Many people move to English-speaking countries such as the United States.

Fitting In

You and your parents may be new to the English-speaking country. You've probably met lots of kids at school. You are learning English. You might want to fit in. You may start to feel **embarrassed** (em-BAYR-est) that your family eats different foods, wears different clothes, or speaks a different language. But fitting in doesn't mean you have to be the same as everyone else. You can be proud of the customs of the country you and your parents come from. Being different is what makes us interesting to each other.

Your school is made up of many different kinds of kids. ▶

Learning English

You can learn a new language more easily than your parents can. You go to school, so you hear English a lot. At school, you learn to speak, read, and write in English. You watch television, read books, and have friends who speak English. You can **practice** (PRAK-tiss) your English often. Your English is probably very good. But it may be much harder for your parents to learn English.

◀ You have a chance to practice your new language with your English-speaking friends.

Many Reasons

There are many reasons why your parents may not have learned to speak English. Many parents work long days. They don't have time to learn a new language. Other families live in an area filled with people who speak the same language they do. These parents might not have had to learn English to do everyday things in that area. And some parents may not want to learn a new language. They might be too proud or scared to try to speak a new language in front of other people.

Many people move from China to areas such as Chinatown, ▶ where many people speak the same langauge they do.

How This Can Affect You

If your parent does not speak English, it can put a lot of **pressure** (PREH-sher) on you. You may not be able to share or talk about some of the things that are going on in your life. Your mom may not be able to understand what your doctor says at your checkup. Your dad might not be able meet with your teacher or understand your lines in the school play. You may need to **translate** (TRANZ-layt) if your parent asks for something in a store or gets a letter in the mail.

◄ You may have to translate important papers, such as your report card, for your parent.

Mixed Feelings

You may have mixed feelings about your parent. You may feel sad that you can't share everything that's going on in your life with your parents. You may also feel as though you have to help your parents because they don't speak English. But you may also be angry about the extra things that you have to do. You may have to act more grown-up than your friends do. Acting more grown-up can make you feel important. But it can also make you feel **resentful** (ree-ZENT-ful).

Sometimes resentment can turn into anger toward your parent. ▶

Talking It Out

The best way to deal with all the things you're feeling is to talk about them. Telling your parent how you feel may help you feel better. If you don't want to talk to your parent, there are other adults you can talk to. Try talking to a teacher, school counselor, minister, rabbi, or a friend's parent. Talking about your feelings can help you understand them. It can also help you find ways to deal with things that you may not be able to change, such as your parent not knowing English.

◀ Talking to someone may help you learn to deal with your feelings.

Helping Your Parent

Your parents may be willing to learn English with some help from you. There are many ways to help someone learn to speak a language. Speak English to your parent in simple, easy sentences. Point to different things around the house, and say their names in your parent's language. Then say the name in English. Ask your parent to watch television with you. Read books in English to your parent. These are good ways to spend time with your parents and help them learn English.

Teaching your parent English is one way you and your parent can spend some time together. ▶

It's Your Parent's Decision

Your parents may decide not to learn English. If this is the case, you have to learn to **accept** (ak-SEPT) their decision. This means that you may have to help your parents in some ways. You may feel sad or angry about their decision. It will help to talk to someone about how you feel.

◀ Your parent's decision not to learn English may make things a little harder for you. But your parent still loves you and wants the best for you.

Sharing

Sometimes kids begin to forget the language their parents speak. This can make it hard for kids and parents to talk to and understand each other. One way to keep this from happening is to share things with each other. As you teach your parents new words in English, let your parents teach you new words in their language. Take some time to learn more about the country you and your parents come from. It's important to understand and be able to talk to people you love.

Glossary

accept (ak-SEPT) To learn to deal with or agree with.

custom (KUS-tum) A way of doing something that is passed down from parent to child.

embarrass (em-BAYR-ess) To make uneasy and ashamed.

foreign (FOR-en) Having to do with other countries.

practice (PRAK-tiss) To do over and over to get better at something.

pressure (PREH-sher) Stress or strain.

resentful (ree-ZENT-ful) Feeling angry.

tradition (truh-DISH-un) The beliefs, customs, and stories passed down from parent to child.

translate (TRANZ-layt) To change from one language to another.

Index